LONDON MIDLAND STEAM in the East Midlands

LONDON MIDLAND
STEAM
IN THE EAST MIDLANDS

J. F. HENTON

D. BRADFORD BARTON LIMITED

Frontispiece: Stanier Class 5 No. 45267 pulls away past clear signals from its stop at Trent on an express from Bradford to St. Pancras in March 1954.

 © *copyright D. Bradford Barton Ltd 1975*   ISBN *0 85153 207 1*

printed in Great Britain by Chapel River Press (IPC Printers), Andover

for the publishers

D. BRADFORD BARTON LTD · Trethellan House · Truro · Cornwall · England

introduction

Nationalisation in 1948 was the start of an interesting period for railway enthusiasts and photographers due to the many changes that came about, such as locomotive re-numbering, experimental liveries and regional boundary alterations, all this at a time when management was endeavouring to cope with these new conditions whilst still suffering from the effect of post-war shortages and restrictions. Commencing with various examples of trains in LMS style, this volume illustrates some of the changes that developed in the East Midlands in the post-war years. As people again began to enjoy themselves—yet with petrol rationing still in force and few new cars—holiday and excursion traffic boomed, so that at weekends and Bank Holiday periods heavy and frequent trains to a great variety of destinations followed each other in quick succession.

The photographs cover the area surrounding Derby and Nottingham centred on that original complex of lines and junctions known as Trent. Busy and important though this was, it consisted only of a large, solitary island platform set amongst fields, approached in 1948 by either an unmade road or an ash footpath, this latter involving a walk of over a mile from Long Eaton, the nearest centre of habitation. We also take a look at passenger and freight traffic farther up the Erewash Valley, a busy line with four tracks all the way from Toton to north of Chesterfield, fed by numerous colliery branches which—in the days before much use of oil fuel—ensured a procession of loaded coal trains as well as their respective empty workings. Also included are scenes on the fringe of the M & GN, that long, mainly single track line, stretching from Saxby Junction through South Lynn to the coastal resorts of Norfolk. Summer Saturdays saw this route over-burdened with holiday extras converging on Saxby from the East Midlands, eventually meeting the return workings, when a matter of a few minutes delay could snowball into massive deficits of time on an August Saturday.

In 1948, 'Jubilee' and Stanier Class 5 4-6-0s were the standard first line passenger motive power, still assisted on occasions by Compound 4-4-0s. Local trains were in the hands of ex-Midland Class 2 4-4-0s or Fowler and Stanier 2-6-4 tanks. Freight traffic was handled by Stanier 2-8-0s and Garratts plus a multitude of Midland type 0-6-0s, many of which lasted almost until the end of steam in the area. With coal still the main industrial and domestic fuel, there was a constant procession of coal trains south to Cricklewood for London and the south-east, to Peterborough for the eastern counties and via Castle Donington to Birmingham and the south-west. The trains of returning empties regularly had to queue up before they could be accepted into the large and busy Toton marshalling yards, situated on the Erewash Valley line just north of Trent. From the south and the Nottingham direction there were separate high level lines provided, so keeping clear of passenger trains in the Trent station area.

The whole of this district was rich in things Midland—stations, signal boxes, level crossings and a host of the distinctive signals and the photographs illustrate the gradual change in these over the years until the demise of steam in the locality.

October 1948 sees Compound 4-4-0, renumbered 41021 but with its tender still lettered LMS, marshalling its train at Derby. The station still retains part of its overall roof, though showing signs of bomb damage during the war. One of the few remaining Class 3 4-4-0s stands in the bay platform.

'Jubilee' Class No. 5696 *Arethusa*, with L M S lettering and number, alongside Platform 3 of Nottingham's Midland station at the head of a Manchester–St. Pancras express. This was one of the 'Jubilees' fitted with a Fowler style of narrow tender.

For many years both large and small Tilbury 4-4-2Ts worked the local service from Nottingham to Mansfield, rarely getting on to any other routes. Here, No. 41940 awaits departure from Nottingham for Mansfield and Worksop on a sunny evening in June 1948.

Another 'Jubilee', No. 5648 *Wemyss*, still in L M S livery, coasts into Beeston station, on the Sunday 3.40 p.m. express from Nottingham to St. Pancras, August 1947.

In September 1949, rebuilt 'Royal Scot' No. 46112 *Sherwood Forester*, specially prepared, came light from Crewe for the unveiling of its new nameplate and Regimental crest. Here it is seen being positioned before the official dais on Platform 6 at Nottingham.

Although basically an LMS design by Ivatt in 1947, 2-6-0 No. M3010 was a sign of the standard engines to come. The M prefix and British Railways in full on the tender were short-lived. No. M3010 with its double chimney makes an energetic start from Derby on an afternoon train to Crewe in September 1948.

'Jubilee' No. 45694 *Bellerophon*, soon after leaving Trent station on the down Sunday 'Thames–Clyde Express', passes North Erewash Junction on its way northwards. The sidings and wagons on the right originated as Clay's wagon works in Midland days and are still in business albeit under new owners.

In the sunlight of an evening in May 1949, Compound 4-4-0 No. 41057 stands under the bridge carrying the ex-Great Central line at Nottingham awaiting departure time on an all-stations local to Derby.

1948 saw the invasion of Midland territory for the first time by regular daily workings with Eastern Region locomotives. The through Cleethorpes–Birmingham train was worked throughout by a B1 4-6-0, and No. 61318 is seen leaving Trent in July 1950 for its next stop at Loughborough en route to Birmingham. On the down main line, Class 4 0-6-0 No. 44583 stands awaiting the road.

Midland Class 2 4-4-0 No. 40541, with front numberplates missing after diversion for Sunday engineering work, crosses back to the correct line at Attenborough on a Nottingham–Leicester train in July 1949. The pilotman who had accompanied the train can be seen on the station platform waiting to cross to the signal box to await a return trip to Beeston.

In June 1949
Nottingham celebrated
its quincentenary
and was visited by
the then Princess
Elizabeth and Duke
of Edinburgh. The
Royal Train spent the
night on the north
curve at Trent and is
seen here near
Beeston heading
sedately towards
Nottingham behind
Class 5 4-6-0
No. 44662.

British Rail
experimented from
time to time with
various locomotives
and coach liveries,
and in 1948 ran
complete trains on
various regions. The
4.50 p.m. from
St. Pancras to
Bradford is seen here
running into
Nottingham with
'Jubilee' No. 45565
Victoria painted
green at the head of a
train in what was
christened 'plum and
spilt milk' livery.
In those early post-war
days, this was indeed
a welcome sight.

A Class 4F 0-6-0, with the number 4223 chalked on the smokebox, tops Wollaton summit between Nottingham and Trowell on a hot afternoon in July 1949, heading for stations up the Erewash Valley with a returning holiday extra.

On a misty morning in February 1950, Stanier Class 5 No. 45056 passes through the cutting near Hasland on a Bradford–St. Pancras express. The cold weather and a good fire make for a near perfect exhaust.

Stanier 2-8-0
No. 48538 slows to
take the relief line past
Trent station on a
Derby–Toton freight,
8 July 1950.

On the last lap of its journey, Class 4 0-6-0 No. 44034 passes Sheet Stores Junction on a Yarmouth–Derby Saturdays-only train in July 1950. Note the tablet catcher on the tender which would find use whilst the train was travelling over the M & GN section. The lines in the right foreground are those to Stenson Junction via Castle Donington.

Another Class 4 0-6-0, still unrenumbered No. 4224, trundles through the snow in December 1950 with coal empties on its way from Birmingham to Toton. The locomotive is passing the signal controlling the branch to Melbourne and Ashby.

18

Another Yarmouth–Derby train entering Platform 6 at Nottingham behind Class 4 Nos. 4419 and 43937. The leading engine is LMS built and the second of superheated Midland design, each with their own distinctive style of tender.

'Jubilee' No. 45573 *Newfoundland* hurries a Bradford–St. Pancras express across the river Trent towards Redhill Tunnel in October 1953. This was the site of the original Midland Counties bridge, the goods line bridge on the right being built later.

The 2.00 p.m. St. Pancras–Bradford express near Wollaton behind 'Jubilee' No. 45604 *Ceylon*, in April 1951. The fireman is taking a breather before the train drops downgrade to Trowell Junction after which the steady climb up the Erewash Valley will require his efforts again for more steam.

A grimy 'Jubilee', No. 45627 *Sierra Leone*, accelerating a Sunday Manchester–St. Pancras express away from Trent on a cold March morning in 1951, passing under the bridge carrying the high level goods lines to Toton.

A hot Sunday afternoon in June 1951 sees the 3.40 p.m. Nottingham–St. Pancras starting away from the stop at Beeston headed by Class 5 No. 44658.

Class 4 0-6-0 No. 44122 with tender cab, takes the sharp curve at Long Eaton Junction on a Beeston to ...oton coal train. Usually these trains took the high level route up to Meadow Lane Junction to avoid the ...wo busy level crossings in Long Eaton.

'Jubilee' No. 45680 *Camperdown* brings its train from Manchester very gingerly off the north curve into Trent station in August 1951. The handsome Midland signal gantry lasted to the end of manual signalling in the area.

Fowler 2-6-4T No. 42333 coasts past London Road Junction at Nottingham, in September 1951, on the 1.55 p.m. stopping train from Melton Mowbray. The three-arm Midland signal controlled the passenger and goods lines; the latter ran round the back of the station and the metals have now been lifted, the area having been made into part of the station car park.

On Sundays during the 1950s, the St. Pancras–Glasgow express stopped at Trent shortly after noon for passengers to and from Nottingham and Derby, each of which provided connecting trains. Midland Compound No. 41000, in a filthy condition, sets off from Derby past the locomotive shed on its short non-stop run to Trent on this duty in 1951.

Stanier Class 5 No. 44825 has the distant signal against it at Lenton South Junction, Nottingham, barely a mile on its journey on the 1.25 p.m. semi-fast to St. Pancras.

Derby shed has provided a commendably clean and well-coaled 'Jubilee', No. 45585 *Hyderabad*, to take over a Newcastle–Bristol express, seen here taking the West of England line from its home station in May 1952.

tanier Class 8 No. 48280 approaching Sheet Stores Junction in March 1952 on a Toton-Washwood Heath coal train. Visible over the wagons is another coal train heading south to Redhill Tunnel.

Class 4 No. 44142, on a Derby–Beeston freight, turns off towards Trent at Sheet Stores Junction in March 1952. The somewhat unusual name of this junction came from the buildings just in view over the end of the train, being the works where from Midland days tarpaulins or wagon sheets were made and repaired.

Almost from new No. 45656 *Cochrane* was shedded at Nottingham (16A) and this 'Jubilee' was a regular visitor to Trent station, but when this photograph was taken in February 1952 it had been transferred to Millhouses shed, Sheffield (19B) and was making its stop at Trent on a Sunday Bradford–St. Pancras express.

In June 1952 the Stephenson Locomotive Society ran a rail tour from Derby over a number of branch lines in the area. The three-coach train was hauled by Midland 0-4-4T No. 58087 and is seen here heading round the north curve out of Trent station on its way back to Derby.

By 1952, BR Standard Class 5 4-6-0s had arrived in the area. At first there seemed to be doubt in some quarters whether they would match up to the Stanier counterparts but practice seemed to prove that they could; No. 73017 leaves Trent on a semi-fast from Nottingham to St. Pancras.

This rear view of 'Jubilee' No. 45616 *Malta GC* shows clearly the difference in width between locomotive and tender when coupled to a Fowler instead of the more usual Stanier variety. It is seen heading the lunch-time express out of Nottingham up the Melton line en route to Kettering and St. Pancras in July 1952.

Fairburn 2-6-4T No. 42185 with a train from Lincoln, stopping at all stations, restarting after a signal check outside Nottingham station. On the left can be seen part of one of the platforms of London Road Low Level station, now used as a parcels depot.

During the 1950s, the down 'Thames–Clyde Express' was regularly piloted from Leicester to Sheffie by a Compound 4-4-0—not for reason of the load but purely for operating purposes. The express seen passing Coates Park South signal box, near Alfreton, with No. 41089 piloting No. 455◆ *Queensland.* The effect of mining subsidence, which so bedevilled the Erewash Valley line, can b distinctly seen by its effect on the first few coaches of the train.

The NCB sank a new colliery at Calverton, north of Nottingham, and a new rail line was made connecting with the MR Mansfield branch as well as to the GNR Leen Valley line, all double-tracked with quite extensive signalling. All this proved to be somewhat optimistic as the branch was soon singled, the Leen Valley saw little traffic and, in fact, both the junction and its track have been lifted, leaving the only connection to the LMR. On 27 April 1957, the SLS ran a rail tour which covered this branch, seen here by Calverton Colliery signal box behind Standard 2-6-2T No. 84006.

Stanton Ironworks, near Ilkeston, covers a large area and had connections with both the MR and GNR systems, with numerous access routes and sidings. Class 4 0-6-0 No. 44154 is seen here passing through part of the works complex on a coal train in August 1958.

Class 5 No. 44825 accelerates a Nottingham–St. Pancras express away from Trent on a winter's day in 1952.

Another SLS rail tour in April 1956 traversed various branches in Nottinghamshire and Derbyshire; on this occasion 2-6-2T No. 84008 pauses for water at Codnor Park station on the Erewash Valley line.

'Jubilee' No. 45636 *Uganda* passing under the high level goods lines on the approach to Trent with the Sunday 3.40 p.m. express from Nottingham to St. Pancras. The clear signal on the opposite line is for an up express from Derby, so that in a few moments both trains will be standing in Trent station, facing opposite directions, but both going to the same destination. This was always one of the peculiarities that the maze of lines around Trent could produce to confuse the casual traveller.

41

In 1956 the RCTS annual rail tour 'The East Midlander' travelled to Swindon works and was hauled throughout by Class 2 4-4-0 No. 40454, a journey this old locomotive, after special preparation by the local shed staff, performed with distinction. Here the train awaits departure from Nottingham. Note the hand coaling on the tender, reminiscent of Midland days.

A Sheffield–Derby stopping train hauled by Class 4 No. 43859 at Stretton in August 1956. This is part of Stephenson's North Midland line and the platforms here are partially staggered.

Class 4 No. 44427 makes heavy weather with a load of coal from Toton as it negotiates the curves through Trent station; the splitting distant signal indicates a clear road on to the Castle Donington line at Sheet Stores Junction.

Another of that most common class, the 4F 0-6-0, this time No. 43943, emerging from Redhill Tunnel on the down goods line with coal empties for Toton and about to cross the bridge over the River Trent. When the goods lines were opened, the castellated entrance was built to match the earlier passenger lines which are out of sight to the right.

Fowler 2-6-4T No. 42361 crossing the River Trent at the head of a Nottingham–Leicester stopping train in May 1955. Comparison of this photograph with that on page 20 shows the replacement of the original attractively curved girders of the bridge with gaunt angular beams, no doubt ensuring strength but not beauty.

Horwich 'Crab' 2-6-0 No. 42797 takes the curve at Long Eaton Junction to head up the Erewash Valley line on a Bank Holiday excursion from Nottingham to Belle Vue. When not used for freight work, these locomotives were ideal for excursion and holiday traffic.

During August 1955, dynamometer car trials were carried out to evaluate certain low grade coal. 'Patriot' Class 4-6-0 No. 45506 *The Royal Pioneer Corps* was borrowed for the job and here makes a slow smoky start on the 8.20 a.m. semi-fast to St. Pancras.

To serve the ironstone workings in the uplands north-east of Melton Mowbray, both the M R and G N R built freight lines to bring out the ore. The M R constructed such a line from the ironworks at Holwell on the Nottingham–Kettering route on which was included a timber viaduct, unusual for this area. When the photograph was taken, filling in caused Class 4 0-6-0 No. 44480 to take its train of ore across very cautiously.

Compound 4-4-0 No. 40929 takes its empty stock to the London Road carriage sidings at Nottingham after working a stopping train from Derby, September 1955.

Another regular ER working that developed in the 1950s was the use by Lincoln shed of ex-G C Directors' on certain through Lincoln–Derby trains. Here D 11 4-4-0 No. 62663 *Prince Albert* leaves Trent on the last lap of the journey to Derby in April 1955.

Beyer-Garratt 2-6-0 + 0-6-2 No.47971 gathers speed downgrade from the high level goods lines with a Toton–Brent coal train in May 1955. These handsome and powerful locomotives worked regularly in the area and the tempo of their exhaust from front and rear cylinders provided considerable discussion in the popular railway press for many years.

Fowler 2-6-4T No.42361 leaving Attenborough with a Nottingham–Leicester train on a sunny morning in January 1954.

The main modern freight locomotive in post-war years was the Stanier 8F 2-8-0; No.48112, from Toton shed, heads southwards on a freight train on the high level goods line, which allowed the intensive workings to avoid Trent station and the double track section through Long Eaton with its busy level crossings.

The Bradford–St. Pancras express that left Nottingham in mid-afternoon was always a popular train and, with only slight alterations to timings, ran for many years. 'Jubilee' No. 45650 *Blake* sets out up the Kettering line on this working in March 1953.

Stanier Class 5 No. 44828 hurries a Bradford–St. Pancras express through Long Eaton station and its level crossing on a Sunday afternoon in February 1953.

In April 1953 the S L S organised a tour over the Cromford and High Peak line with a connecting special shuttle service between Duffield and Wirksworth. Midland 0-4-4T No. 58077 arrives in the branch platform at Duffield on one of these workings.

The main line southwards from Nottingham towards Kettering climbs at a gradient of 1 in 100 fo approximately ten miles. In May 1953, 'Jubilee' No. 45579 *Punjab* on a Bradford–St. Pancras expres takes this in its stride through the closed Edwalton station. The site is now derelict, with buildings an signals razed to the ground and just the ballast bed remaining. South from Edwalton is the limit of te track for the new high-speed trains.

'Crab' 2-6-0 No. 42839 slows for London Road Junction at Nottingham on a Somers Town–Leeds freight, February 1953.

A popular outing in both pre- and post-war years was a half-day excursion to London. Stanier Class 5 No. 44776, on one of these workings from Derby on Whit Sunday 1953, passes Long Eaton Junction en route via Nottingham and Kettering to St. Pancras. The tall Midland signal shows 'line clear' into Trent, the left hand arms being for the goods line and right hand for the curve round to Long Eaton and the Erewash Valley line.

On August Bank holiday 1953 a grimy Class 5 No. 44845 eases out of Platform 1 at Nottingham on to the Lincoln line with a through Newstead to Cleethorpes holiday excursion.

Compound 4-4-0 No. 41060 darkens the sky as it leaves Trent on a through train from Lincoln to Derby in June 1953.

aprotti versions of the Stanier Class 5 were not common in the East Midlands; No. 44745 lays a trail of ack smoke across the countryside on the approach to Breadsall crossing with a relief Bristol to Leeds press in August 1953.

Two views of Compound 4-4-0 No. 41077 on a Derby–St. Pancras excursion, made up of Eastern Region stock, in August 1953. Above, it is shown entering the platform at Trent station round the sharp north curve and (left) setting off on the main line towards Leicester.

An unusual local empty stock working was to bring the coach used on the Rolleston Junction to Southwell push-and-pull service to Nottingham for cleaning; ex-MR 0-4-4T No. 58056 sets off from Nottingham non-stop to Rolleston Junction with its one empty coach in August 1953.

Compound 4-4-0 No. 41051, on a relief up express from Nottingham, accelerates away from Trent on its way south in August 1953. Below, Midland Class 2 No. 40546 heading a Nottingham–Derby stopping train past Lenton South Junction, May 1951.

Class 4 No. 44313 opens up after the slack through Trent station with a southbound freight from Beeston sidings routed on the up main line in October 1953.

'Jubilee' No. 45616 *Malta GC* takes the Erewash Valley line after the stop at Trent with a St. Pancras–Bradford express on an overcast day in March 1954. Below, a common sight in the Trent area was down freight trains awaiting their turn for acceptance into Toton marshalling yard; Stanier 2-8-0 No. 48037 quietly waits at Meadow Lane Junction with a train of empties.

Another 'Jubilee', No. 45557 *New Brunswick*, heading a down express out of Nottingham past London Road Junction signal box on a hot summer day in 1954.

Midland Class 3 0-6-0 No. 43826 passing briskly through Trent station heading fo Birmingham with a coal train from Toton in April 1954.

Coal traffic generally travelled up the Erewash Valley line to Toton, but sometimes loaded trains worked northwards, as shown here with Class 0-6-0 No. 43550 passing Coates Park South on 9 September 1955.

Stanier Class 5 No. 44848 starting away from Attenborough on a stopping train from Nottingham to Leeds on a Saturday in January 1954.

Midland Class 2 4-4-0s were rarely seen on freight workings, but No. 40493 has been called on to work the Nottingham–Derby (St. Marys) fitted freight one after noon in July 1954 and is seen here passing Attenborough.

An ex-Great Eastern D 16 4-4-0 would indeed have aroused surprise a decade earlier in this normally Midland area, but in April 1957 it was common enough, as Lincoln shed was using these locomotives on through workings to Derby. Here, No. 62571 leaves Nottingham on an afternoon return working. Part of London Road Low Level station can be seen on the right.

Ample power for a four coach Derby–Nottingham train as Compound No. 4092 pilots 2-6-4T No. 42174, seen on the curve from Sheet Stores Junction into Trent station.

It was always interesting to travel into Derby by train from the Trent direction, as one slowly passed by the locomotive shed, and this scene taken in September 1954, with Compound No. 41064 on the turntable, was basically unchanged over a period of many years.

A commendably clean 'Austerity' 2-8-0, No. 90190, heads an up coal train on the main Erewash Valley line between Coates Park North and South boxes, May 1958.

A typical scene on the M & GN line; on 2 August 1958, a Yarmouth–Leicester train
waits at Little Bytham Junction for its turn to enter the single line section ahead.

Earlier on the same day, Class 4 0-6-0s Nos. 44231 and 44423 approach Saxby on the 9.00 a.m. Yarmouth–Birmingham train. The Midland main line from Nottingham to Kettering curves away to the right.

The 12.05 p.m. train from Nottingham to Leeds, whilst invariably hauled by a tender locomotive, could vary from a 'Jubilee' to a Class 4 0-6-0, as shown here heading northwards past Coates Park South behind No. 43958 in May 1958.

Also on 2 August 1958, Class 0-6-0 No. 44419 takes the single line of the M & GN from Saxby at the head of a Derby–Yarmouth and Cromer train. Below, BR Standard 4-6-0 No. 75058 stands in Platform 5 at Nottingham after arriving on an all stations train from Kettering, May 1958.

In 1959 Nottingham Forest Football Club went to Wembley for the cup final and amongst the many extra special trains run that day was one for the Club headed by rebuilt 'Royal Scot' No. 46158 *The Loyal Regiment*, seen here passing through West Bridgford on its way to St. Pancras.

When this photograph was taken on 30 April 1959, the Erewash Valley line was still busy enough to warrant both fast and slow lines; Class 5 No. 44944 piloting 'Jubilee' No. 45677 *Beatty* on an up express is overtaking Class 8 No. 48185 heading a coal train on the up slow line.

Standard Class 5 No.73170 makes a lively exit from Nottingham taking the Kettering line with a relie
express from Sheffield to St. Pancras in August 1958.

This photograph clearly shows the rural aspect around Trent station as 'Jubilee' No.45667 *Jellicoe*
pauses on its way to St. Pancras with an express from Nottingham, 14 June 1959.

To its end Midland Region 0-4-4Ts worked the push-and-pull service from Southwell to Rolleston Junction. Here No. 58065 approaches Upton Crossing on an afternoon working in May 1959. Southwell station can be faintly discerned in the background, after which the branch became single track and was freight only. All this is now closed and the track lifted.

After its withdrawal in September 1951, British Railways restored Midland Compound 4-4-0 in 1959 to as near its original condition as possible, repainted in Midland livery and numbered 1000. In August of that year, the SLS sponsored a special train from Birmingham to Doncaster and York, using the restored Compound to haul the train— seen here at Derby on the way northwards.

Class 5 No. 45147 slows for the stop at Trent station in April 1960 on a Northampton–Bradford Sunday Excursion. A Nottingham portion will be added to the rear, making it up to a ten-coach train.

Stanier Class 8F2 No. 48271 approaching Trent Junction on the up goods line on 16 April 1960, heading a Carlisle-London fitted freight. This was normally a Class 5 turn, suggesting (as No. 48271 is a Toton locomotive) that there had been a failure of the regular one booked for this train.

In June 1962, Long Eaton station was still open and presented a typically Midland appearance with its gated level crossing and attractive signals showing line clear right through to Trent station for the up 'Thames–Clyde Express'.

A few minutes later, the express coasts through Long Eaton station from its previous stop at Sheffield behind BR 'Britannia' Pacific No. 70053 *Moray Firth*.

Two views of Trent station from the south with the goods lines on the right. Above, 'Jubilee' No. 45620 *North Borneo* has passed the station on the platform avoiding line with a Nottingham–St. Pancras excursion in April 1960. Below, a few days later, rebuilt 'Royal Scot' No. 46160 *Queen Victoria's Rifleman* starts away from the station on the way to St. Pancras with an express from Leeds and Bradford.

Stanier 2-6-4T No. 42636 awaits departure from Platform 3 at Nottingham station on the 12.25 Saturdays-only train to Melton Mowbray, May 1961.

Stanier Class 5 No. 45088 moves off from Derby station under clear signals heading a Bristol–Bradford relief express in September 1962. A sign of things to come is the diesel standing in the background.

In its latter days, the famous No. 46100 *Royal Scot* worked on the Midland Division and is seen here on a Sunday morning in September 1962 at Nottingham shed in company with one of the Horwich Moguls.

One of the many
2-8-0s, No. 48164, on a
train consisting
mainly of coal, heads
northwards on the
Erewash Valley line
past Coates Park
South, April 1960.

BR 9F 2-10-0 No.92089 creeps slowly round the 'back road' at Trent station with a down load of iron ore in May 1965. Track lifting has already started for the redesigning of the layout here. Comparison of this photograph with that on page 80 shows that a rural aspect surrounded Trent on all sides.

At the same locality in August 1963, Class 4 0-6-0 No.44054 heads a train of condemned wagons northwards.

Class 4 No. 43994, working wrong line, stands with a p.w. train on the Nottingham–Kettering line in West Bridgford on 7 August 1964. This main line, condemned by Dr. Beeching, was not to see service much longer, and is now lifted.

In May 1965, the Warwickshire Railway Society organised a rail tour to the Nottingham district hauled by 9F 2-10-0 No. 92155, photographed here taking the goods only line at Lenton South Junction leading to the North Junction and the Mansfield branch.

The 'Midland Requiem'—a rail tour organised by the RCTS—ran from Birmingham to the Nottingham area in October 1965. This was a salute and farewell to the 4F 0-6-0s which for so many years seemed a permanent part of railway operation in the area. Here, No. 43953 waits at Sheet Stores Junction for its path through Trent.

Standard 9F 2-10-0 No. 92153 heading for the south-west towards Birmingham after joining the main line from Derby at Stenson Junction with a coal train from Toton, April 1960.

The Railway Enthusiasts Club tour in July 1966 travelled over a number of colliery branches and was composed of a train of fitted brake vans, although under express headlamps. The passengers travelled by ordinary service to Trent where the special started; it is seen here leaving on the line towards Nottingham headed by specially cleaned Class 5 No. 44825.

What must have been one of the last sights of steam in the area was on 6 April 1968, when 9F 2-10-0 No. 92203 and Standard Class 4 No. 75029 were *en route* south passing Trent Junction, having been purchased by the well known railway artist David Shepherd.